Tell Me Why

WHY?

Skunks Smell Bad

Susan H. Gray

Published in the United States of America by Cherry Lake Publishing
Ann Arbor, Michigan
www.cherrylakepublishing.com

Content Adviser: Dr. Stephen S. Ditchkoff, Professor of Wildlife Sciences, Auburn University,
Auburn, Alabama
Reading Adviser: Marla Conn, Readability, Inc.

Photo Credits: © PathDoc/Shutterstock Images, cover, 1, 5; © michaeljung/Shutterstock Images,
cover, 1, 9; © xavier gallego morell/Shutterstock Images, cover, 1, 19; © Critterbiz/Shutterstock
Images, cover, 1; © Heiko Kiera/Shutterstock Images, cover, 1, 5, 9; © Dennis W. Donohue/
Shutterstock Images, cover, 1; © Ingram Publishing/Thinkstock, 7; © Cynthia Kidwell/Shutterstock
Images, 11; © Geoffrey Kuchera/Shutterstock Images, 13, 17; © Holly Kuchera/Thinkstock, 15;
© Sari ONeal/Shutterstock Images, 19; ©Teerapun Fuangtong/Thinkstock, 21

Library of Congress Cataloging-in-Publication Data

Gray, Susan Heinrichs, author.
  Skunks smell bad / by Susan H. Gray.
      pages cm. -- (Tell me why)
  Summary: "Young children are naturally curious about animals. Tell Me Why
Skunks Smell Bad offers answers to their most compelling questions about
when skunks attack. Age-appropriate explanations and appealing photos
encourage readers to continue their quest for knowledge. Additional text
features and search tools, including a glossary and an index, help students
locate information and learn new words."—Provided by publisher.
  Audience: Ages 6-10.
  Audience: K to grade 3.
  ISBN 978-1-63188-999-8 (hardcover) -- ISBN 978-1-63362-038-4 (pbk.) --
ISBN 978-1-63362-077-3 (pdf) -- ISBN 978-1-63362-116-9 (ebook) 1.
Skunks--Juvenile literature. 2. Animal chemical defenses--Juvenile
literature. 3. Adaptation (Biology)--Juvenile literature. I. Title.

QL737.C248G73 2015
599.76'8--dc23

2014025718

Cherry Lake Publishing would like to acknowledge the work of The Partnership for 21st Century
Skills. Please visit www.21.org for more information.

Printed in the United States of America
Corporate Graphics

Table of Contents

Phew-Eee!

Emily heard something scratching around in her dad's garden. Was it a rabbit or a turtle? Emily just had to find out.

It was already getting dark outside. Emily squinted her eyes as she drew near the garden. Suddenly, a little head poked out from behind a plant. The mysterious animal crept out a little farther. Then it began moving strangely.

Have your friends or neighbors ever seen a skunk? If they have, ask them if it was during the day or at night.

Skunks often live in neighborhoods, near people's houses.

All of a sudden, a terrible **stench** filled the air. Emily shut her eyes tightly and held her breath. She turned and began running back to the house. She couldn't see where she was going and ran right into her dad.

"Dad! There's a skunk in the garden!" she shouted. "Yuck! Why do they smell so bad?"

Emily and her dad went inside. Soon her dad called to her. "Emily, look what I found about skunks on the Internet!"

The smell of a skunk will make you want to hold your nose!

A Helpless Animal?

Emily's dad began to read aloud. "Skunks live in open fields and in brushy or wooded areas. They also live in farmlands and along riverbanks. Sometimes, they even appear in town. These little **mammals** eat whatever they can find. They dig in the earth to find worms and **grubs**. They scratch through the grass for crickets and beetles. They also eat mice, eggs, corn, berries, and pet food."

Her dad stopped reading. "Now there's a good reason to keep pet food inside!" he laughed.

LOOK!

What features would help this skunk find worms and insects?

A skunk has a pointed nose and sharp claws.

Her dad continued. "Skunks cannot outrun most **predators**. They cannot leap away from danger.

Her father stopped reading and looked at Emily. "So, they are slow," he said. "They sound like the perfect meal for a predator!"

He went back to reading. "Hawks, owls, foxes, bobcats, **coyotes**, and **cougars** sometimes hunt them. But predators may soon learn that skunks only look helpless."

A full-grown skunk is about the size of a house cat.

Surprise!

A predator that attacks a skunk is in for a shock. When threatened, a skunk boldly faces his **foe**. He arches his back and raises his tail.

These are warning signals. But often, they are completely ignored. Predators that are young don't know what the signals mean. They will continue to threaten the skunk. This is a big mistake!

This bear cub wants to make a new friend, but he'll learn his lesson soon.

The skunk then stamps the ground with his little front feet. This shows that he is getting fed up. Some skunks even do a handstand! This is so they look larger to their enemies. But such actions might not scare predators.

Suddenly, the skunk has had enough. He twists his body around. He points his rear end at the enemy. Then he sprays a foul-smelling oil right at it.

This skunk knows how to send the bear cub away.

The predator jerks backward. His eyes begin to burn. He'll never make that mistake again.

Every skunk is equipped with two **scent glands**. They lie just below the tail and under the skin. Each gland contains some very smelly oil. When threatened, the skunk squirts a mist or a stream of this oil. The ingredients in the oil can temporarily blind an animal. They can also make it feel like vomiting.

If you ever see a skunk in this position, turn around and run.

Stinky, Stinky, Stinky

Skunks are not the only animals that use stench for **defense**. **Opossums** and vultures do this, too. When an opossum senses danger, it sometimes plays dead. It falls over on its side and lies completely still. It also releases green, stinky slime from its rear end. No predator wants to eat such an animal. Once the danger passes, the opossum gets up and goes on its way.

What if opossums were ferocious fighting animals? Would they need to play dead?

This opossum is playing dead.

Vultures use a different method. They love rotten, stinky meat. But when vultures are threatened or need to flee, they don't play dead. They vomit. The stench is enough to send predators running. Plus, it lightens the birds so they can fly away more easily.

Not many animals use stinky defenses. But every animal has some way to protect itself. Zoos are good places to learn how animals behave. Perhaps there is a terrific skunk exhibit near you!

Skunks in a zoo eat a variety of foods including fruits, vegetables, cheese, eggs, worms, and grubs.

Think About It

What if skunks squirted oil that smelled nice? Would predators still leave them alone?

Owls have a poor sense of smell. Would they be likely to attack skunks more than once?

Why might skunks make poor pets?

Glossary

cougars (KOO-gurz) large, tan cats that live in the wild

coyotes (ky-OH-teez) wolflike animals

defense (dih-FENSS) protection

foe (FO) an enemy

grubs (GRUHBZ) young form of some insects that look like short, white worms

mammals (MAM-uhlz) animals that have hair on their bodies and give birth to live young

opossums (uh-POSS-umz) small mammals with a pouch for carrying their young

predators (PREH-duh-turz) animals that hunt and eat other animals

scent glands (SENT GLANDZ) organs that produce foul-smelling chemicals

stench (STENCH) a foul smell or odor

Find Out More

Books:

Gish, Melissa. *Skunks*. Mankato, MN: Creative Paperbacks, 2014.

Lockwood, Sophie. *Skunks*. North Mankato, MN: Child's World, 2008.

Swanson, Diane. *Welcome to the World of Skunks*. Toronto, ON: Whitecap Books, Ltd., 2010.

Web Sites:

National Geographic—Skunk
http://animals.nationalgeographic.com/animals/mammals/skunk/#
Click a button on this site to listen to a sound recording of a skunk.

San Diego Zoo Kids—Skunk
http://kids.sandiegozoo.org/animals/mammals/skunk
Visit this Web site to learn about where skunks live, their food, and their babies.

ZooBorns—Skunk
www.zooborns.com/zooborns/skunk
Here you can see newborn and young skunks and read their stories.

Index

About the Author

Susan H. Gray has a master's degree in zoology. She has worked in research and has taught college-level science classes. Susan has also written more than 140 science and reference books, but especially likes to write about animals. She and her husband, Michael, live in Cabot, Arkansas, with many pets.